COWBOY
ETIQUETTE

TEXAS BIX BENDER

GIBBS SMITH
TO ENRICH AND INSPIRE HUMANKIND
Salt Lake City | Charleston | Santa Fe | Santa Barbara

FOR MADGE AND ALL HER POLITE CRITTERS.

Revised Edition
13 12 11   20 19 18 17 16 15 14 13 12 11 10 9 8 7 6 5 4

Text © 2003 Texas Bix Bender
Animation © 2003 Gibbs Smith, Publisher

Published by
Gibbs Smith
P.O. Box 667
Layton, Utah 84041

1.800.835.4993 orders
www.gibbs-smith.com

Cover design by Black Eye Design
Printed and bound in the U.S.A.
Gibbs Smith books are printed on either recycled, 100% post-
consumer waste, FSC-certified papers or on paper produced from
a 100% certified sustainable forest/controlled wood source.

The Library of Congress has cataloged the earlier edition as follows:

Bender, Texas Bix, 1949–
Cowboy Etiquette / by Texas Bix Bender. — 1st ed.
   p. cm.
ISBN 10: 1-58685-241-8 (first edition)
ISBN 13: 1-58685-241-2 (first edition)
1. Etiquette—Humor. 2. Cowboys—Humor. I. Title.
PN6231.E8 B46 2003

                                        2003010846

ISBN 13: 978-1-4236-0697-0
ISBN 10: 1-4236-0697-3

★ ★ ★

Etiquette *is the difference*

---

between **stable manners**
and **table manners.**

★ ★ ★

**Good etiquette starts
with a smile—**
unless you have something
stuck in your teeth.

★ ★ ★

AT THE TABLE,
*keep your boarding house
reach in check and don't
dribble on your boots.*

★ ★ ★

Nowadays, a lot of folks greet
you with a question:
"What's up?"
"How ya doin'?" or
"How's it goin'?"
The proper cowboy greeting comes
from an awareness of where the sun
is in the sky and consists of the word
"Mornin'," "Afternoon,"
or "Evenin'."

＊　＊　＊

Always tip your
hat to a lady—

AND THEY'RE ALL LADIES.

★ ★ ★

Always raise the toilet seat. And don't forget to set it back down when you're done. In all fairness, cowgirls should raise it up when they get done. This way it's nearly always wrong when you get there, but **good etiquette requires everybody to be fair.**

* * *

IF YOU MAKE A MESS, CLEAN IT UP.

★ ★ ★

Always try to say
the right thing
first thing
after doing
the wrong thing.

★ ★ ★

[*Spurs on the porch* *are borderline.*]

In the house they're over the line.

★ ★ ★

BEING POLITE

means always being a little nicer than you have to be.

★ ★ ★

NEVER

**show your horse more
affection than your wife—**

unless you like sleepin' in the barn.

ACT THE SAME WAY
when you don't have company
as when you do.

★ ★ ★

ACTIN' LIKE YOU'RE BIG

is probably going to have the opposite effect.

★ ★ ★

BRAGGING
IS BAD MANNERS.

* * *

Good manners
go a long way toward
making anybody
more attractive.

★ ★ ★

DUMBASS BUMPER STICKERS on your pickup brand **you** as the **dumbass** who put them there.

* * *

*A man taking
a stand on
high moral
grounds
just might
be standing
on a bluff.*

★ ★ ★

DON'T CUT IN FRONT

AND DON'T CROWD FROM BEHIND.

* * *

AT THE MOVIES:

Take off your hat.

Don't kick the seat in front of you.

Don't talk.

And, for heaven's sake, don't spit.

★ ★ ★

To get a conversation off to a good start,

. . . .

start off with a

. . . .

COMPLIMENT.

★ ★ ★

If you take something without
asking to borrow it,

—— **you stole it.** ——

★ ★ ★

Nowadays some
men like to hug,
slap high fives,
or bump fists
when they meet.

A SIMPLE OLD-FASHIONED HANDSHAKE IS STILL THE COWBOY WAY.

★ ★ ★

Give up your bus seat to a
lady or elderly person—

BEFORE THE BUS GETS TO
WHERE YOU'RE GOIN'.

★ ★ ★

*Most invitations
are specific, not
open-ended.*
So, it ain't polite
*to show up when
everybody else is
leaving and ask,*
"What's for dinner?"

★ ★ ★

If you open a gate,
close it.

If you didn't open it,
close it anyway.

★ ★ ★

If you're waved off,

DON'T GO IN

without a good reason.

* * *

One sign of good manners
is being able to put up with bad ones.

★ ★ ★

Don't talk
with a
full mouth
or an
empty head.

★ ★ ★

KNOWING WHICH FORK TO USE

isn't nearly as important as being good company.

★ ★ ★

When taking a herd through
a populated area,
be sure to
clean up after 'em.

* * *

It's better to
HAVE WORKED
FOR YOUR DINNER

---

than to have dressed for it.

★ ★ ★

**Never start
an argument
at the dinner
table; the least
hungry person
ALWAYS WINS.**

★ ★ ★

If the guests outnumber the chairs, it's called a buffet.

★ ★ ★

If you don't know what to talk about,
TALK ABOUT THREE WORDS—AND THEN SHUT UP.

★ ★ ★

If you've got nothing to say,
· ·
don't take an hour to prove it.

★ ★ ★

When you sit down, lay
your napkin in your lap.

When you get up but
are coming back, leave
it in your chair.

When you're finished,
leave it on the table.

★ ★ ★

DON'T INTERRUPT
unless somebody's hair is on fire.

★ ★ ★

**The only good reason
to leave a party**

---

*without thanking the
host and hostess*

---

is if you weren't invited.

* * *

Never interfere with
another man's dog

unless the dog is about to
**attach himself
to your leg.**

★ ★ ★

**Slurping,
burping, and
gulping are
okay ONLY
when you're alone
with your dog.**
Same goes for
any kind
of licking.

★ ★ ★

Don't use your napkin
to blow your nose!

★ ★ ★

WHITE WINE

is served chilled, in a long-
stemmed glass. That's so you
can hold it by the stem and not
warm the wine with your hand.

RED WINE

is served at room temperature in
a short-stemmed glass. Holding
the wine by the glass itself and
not the stem warms the wine
and releases its flavors.

* * *

BEER

is served in a bottle, but you can
put it in a glass if you want to.

WHISKEY

should never be drunk from the bottle
unless there's no glass around or
you've already had too much to drink.

★ ★ ★

· ·

When served escargot, pour a
little salt on it and forget it.

It will melt while you wait
for the next course.

· ·

★ ★ ★

When you're standing in line,
and it's a long one,

TAKE IT LIKE A MAN.

* * *

If your soup is served too hot,
....
it's not polite for you to blow on it.
....
So, ask your wife to do it.

★ ★ ★

AFTER-DINNER SPEECHES
{ *should be gotten out of the way before dinner.* }

★ ★ ★

WHEN THERE'S NOTHING MORE TO BE SAID, DON'T BE SAYING IT.

* * *

When you've invited your in-laws over for a steak and they show up with a couple of cousins you never heard of and you only have four steaks, cut everybody's meat for 'em.

★ ★ ★

Casual means no tie, but get a haircut, shine your boots, and tuck in your shirttail.

Semiformal means you'll need a tie, a coat, and all of the above.

Black tie formal means you probably don't wanta go.

* * *

STAY HOME IF YOU'RE
CONTAGIOUS.

★ ★ ★

Etiquette is the art of handling yourself – in any situation –

[in a manner that doesn't embarrass you or anyone else]

and lets you keep your sense of humor intact.

* * *

If you're not having fish,
forget the fish fork.
Even if you are having
fish, forget the fish fork.

**One fork's as good as another
unless it's in the road.**

★ ★ ★

When you meet a neighbor on the road, always give him the little one-finger-off-the-wheel salute. **Depending on how you get along with him DETERMINES WHICH FINGER YOU USE.**

* * *

Don't overload your
mouth with opinions.

★ ★ ★

Making someone feel little

makes you look
smaller too.

★ ★ ★

Spills and accidents happen.
DON'T MAKE A BIG DEAL OUT OF 'EM.

★ ★ ★

Sooner or later we all wind up
sitting next to someone at dinner
**who is about as strange as
a duck in Death Valley.**

Good etiquette requires that you
**waddle across the desert with 'em
until dessert is over.**

★ ★ ★

Gossiping is never

GOOD ETIQUETTE.

★　★　★

When you're camping on
somebody else's spread,

LEAVE WITHOUT A TRACE.

★ ★ ★

Don't break your arm
reaching for the
check, but don't sit on
your hands either.

★ ★ ★

[PAY BACK] EVERY FAVOR.

★ ★ ★

WHERE PEOPLE
ARE FROM AND HOW
THEY GOT HERE
HAS GOT NOTHING TO
DO WITH WHERE THEY
SIT AT THE TABLE.

★ ★ ★

SHOW UP FOR DINNER CLEAN AND RESPECTABLY DRESSED.

★ ★ ★

NICKNAMES

are okay if they're
not insults.

Always HOLD THE DOOR FOR A WOMAN—

· · · · · · · · · · · · · · · · ·

or anyone else, for that matter.

★ ★ ★

Give age the respect it deserves—

in people, critters, and whiskey.

★ ★ ★

WOMEN ALWAYS GO FIRST

unless you're going down stairs
or falling off a log.

* * *

It's not **bad luck**
to spill salt,

but tossing it over
your shoulder is a
bad habit.

★ ★ ★

Don't try to pass off
[YOUR PERSONAL LIFE]
as dinner conversation.

★ ★ ★

If a woman spills her drink, hand her a napkin and

LET HER DO THE PATTING.

★ ★ ★

If you make a date,
KEEP IT.

★ ★ ★

Treat **everybody** *like*
they're **important**.

★ ★ ★

KEEP DOWNWIND when approaching a cook wagon so you don't kick up dust on another man's plate.

* * *

DON'T ANSWER

. . . .

the doorbell in your

. . . .

UNDERSHORTS.

★ ★ ★

Don't take the last piece unless you're the last to be served.

('Course, if you've given everybody else a fair chance at it, go ahead and take the last biscuit.)

★ ★ ★

AFTERSHAVE IS NOT

A MARINADE.

★ ★ ★

ON THE TRAIL,

it's all right to fork beans right out of the can, but never drink from the can. It can cut your lips and is an embarrassment to the mules.

* * *

When sharing a can of Vienna
sausages, it's all right to use
your fingers to pull one out,

---

but taking two is rude.

★ ★ ★

WHEN DINING
WITH NUDISTS,

{ *you still must wear
your bandana.* }

★ ★ ★

When somebody asks you to
PASS 'EM A BISCUIT,
they don't mean overhanded.

THE BEST YEAR for any wine is **THE YEAR YOU DRINK IT.**

★ ★ ★

DON'T SERVE UP FAMILY SECRETS
at the dinner table.

* * *

All cowboys are connoisseurs—of horses, dogs, cattle, fences, pickups, saddles, boots, hats, roping, riding, belt buckles, and rodeoing.

(I ain't including women here because it wouldn't be politically correct, and cowboys don't know much about 'em anyway.)

★ ★ ★

Cowboys are also

CONNOISSEURS

OF CUSSIN',

but it just ain't polite to give
public demonstrations.

★ ★ ★

Taste it before you salt it.

★ ★ ★

Politics *and* **religion**
*are hard rolls to chew
on over dinner.*

★ ★ ★

NEVER
go anywhere without your head in your hat.

★ ★ ★

GOOD
NEIGHBORS
don't need fences.

★ ★ ★

A foreman should
approach a hand
with **respect**

if he expects
the hand to show
respect for the work.

* * *

*Give a good day's work
for the wage you sign
on for, and approach
the work with respect,
no matter how tedious.*

★ ★ ★

If you have to tell somebody
yer just kiddin',

maybe yer not.

* * *

If you're the boss, pay
your hires the best wages
you can, not the best wages
you can get away with.

★ ★ ★

{ *Nowadays it's okay for the woman to ask you out–* }
like it was ever up to you anyway.

* * *

At a party,
START SLOW
and
TAPER OFF.

★ ★ ★

IT'S NEVER A MISTAKE
to offer a lady your arm.

★ ★ ★

REMEMBER

that food artfully arranged

has had somebody's fingers all over it.

★ ★ ★

KNOW-IT-ALLS

are a bother to those of us
who really do know it all.

* * *

It's good to know yourself—

but it's not enough.

★ ★ ★

A SMILE
IS ALWAYS
WELCOME.

★ ★ ★

NEVER COMPLAIN— OR BRAG—

to your date about how much you're spending.

★ ★ ★

WHEN IN DOUBT, APOLOGIZE.

★ ★ ★

Avoid frivolity
**in dress
and lawsuits.**

★ ★ ★

It doesn't matter so
much where you sit

as long as you
get fed.

★ ★ ★

When you're invited to dinner,
bring a little something

[*besides your appetite.*]

* * *

If you're on horseback talking
to someone and they're on
the ground, dismount.

IT AIN'T POLITE
TO TALK DOWN TO PEOPLE.

★ ★ ★

NO
WHINING.

★ ★ ★

Two great stress reducers:
I'M SORRY.
I FORGIVE YOU.

* * *

Taking an attitude that
**EVERYBODY'S
OUT TO GET YOU**
just might make everybody
__want__ to get you.

DON'T TAKE OFFENSE

where none was meant.

* * *

**Still the most
important words**
to get along in life:
PLEASE. THANK YOU.

GOOD MANNERS
are like a MasterCard:
they're welcome everywhere you go.

★ ★ ★

Tell folks how to get on,

{ not where to get off. }

★ ★ ★

When you have to go,

don't tell everybody what you're up to.

JUST SAY "EXCUSE ME," AND GO.

* * *

Allow others the
pleasure of payin' you a
compliment

• • • • • • • • • • • •

without **arguin'** about it.

★ ★ ★

Allow that others make
mistakes now and then—
unless you want to be
the only one who ever
tangles his spurs.

★ ★ ★

*If your job is riding
drag in a roundup,*

DON'T TRY TO
TAKE THE POINT.

★ ★ ★

Rules for a Cowboy
in Wine Country

Rule #1: If the host has selected the wine, to insult the wine is to insult the host, so you like it.

Rule #2: Most wines don't need to be taken all that seriously.

Rule #3: Good wine seldom comes with a twist cap.

Rule #4: Wine lingo is not all that hard to master. If you like it, say something like, "Pardner, this doggie is a little wrinkled but stands up to the iron and smooths out well on the palate." If you don't like it, say something like, "Amigo, this pony's legless, has the bouquet of wilted sagebrush, and goes down like yesterday's coffee."

Rule #5: If it's the only bottle of wine, it's always good.

★ ★ ★

Keep your opinion of yourself to yourself.

★ ★ ★

**Sooner or later we
all get our spurs
tangled and trip up.**

**Apologize and do your
best to make it right.**

That's all you can do.

★ ★ ★

A LITTLE SMALL TALK

can say a lot.

★ ★ ★

Eating with
your fingers is okay
if there are no
forks, spoons, or
knives around.
But eating with
someone else's
fingers is
almost **never**
good etiquette.

★ ★ ★

**Don't take your boots off
under the table.
You don't want to compete
with the bouquet of the wine.**

★ ★ ★

It's okay to let yourself
go sometimes.

*Just be sure you can
let yourself back in.*

★ ★ ★

FARTS are not considered
good dinner conversation.